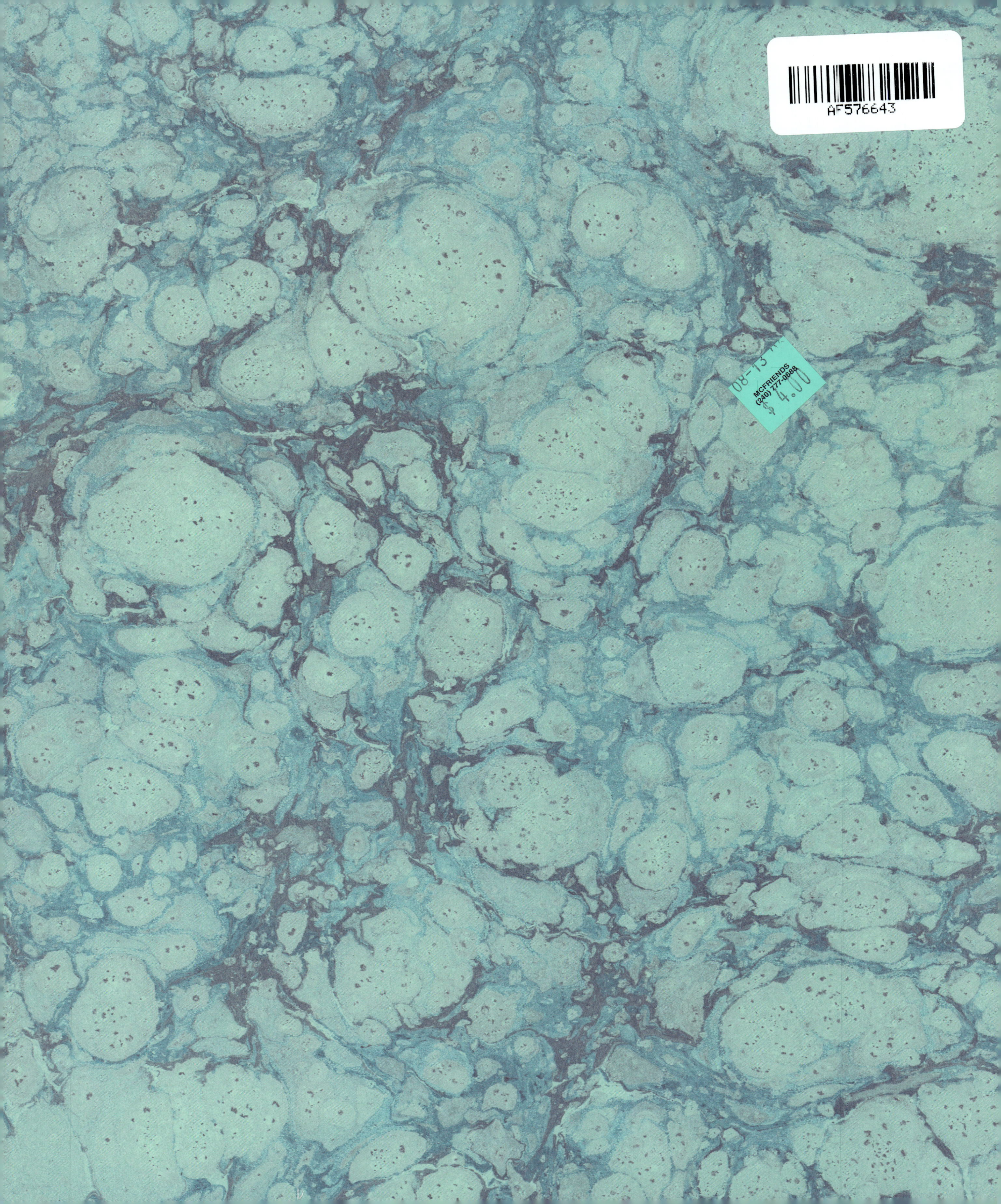

CELEBRATIONS IN ART

AT THE SEA

Celebrations in Art

At the Sea

JENNIFER BRIGHT

MetroBooks

MetroBooks
AN IMPRINT OF FRIEDMAN/FAIRFAX PUBLISHERS

Library of Congress Cataloging-in-Publication Data
Bright, Jennifer
At the sea/Jennifer Bright.
p. cm. -- (Celebrations in art)
ISBN 1-56799-289-7
1. Sea in art. 2. Marine painting. I. Title. II. Series.
N8240.B75 1996
758'.2--dc20 95-50839
CIP

Editor: Elizabeth Viscott Sullivan
Production Editor: Loretta Mowat
Art Director: Jeff Batzli
Designers: Lynne Yeamans and Lori Thorn
Photography Researcher: Samantha Larrance
Production Coordinator: Marnie Ann Boardman

Color separations by HK Scanner Arts Int'l Ltd.
Printed in China by Leefung-Asco Printers Ltd.

For bulk purchases and special sales, please contact:
Friedman/Fairfax Publishers
Attention: Sales Department
15 West 26th Street
New York, NY 10010
212/685-6610 FAX 212/685-1307

Additional Photography Credits: Page 1: Jennifer Bartlett, b. 1941, *At Sands Point #21*, 1986. Oil on canvas, 36" × 84" (91.4 × 213.3cm). Courtesy of Paula Cooper Gallery, Inc., New York. Page 2: Walter Richard Sickert, 1860–1942, *Bathers, Dieppe*, c. 1902. Oil on canvas, 51¾" × 41⅛" (131.4 × 104.4cm). Board of Trustees of the National Museum and Galleries on Mereyside (Walker Art Gallery, Liverpool). Page 3: Unknown, *Meditation by the Sea*, c. 1855. Oil on canvas, 13½" × 19½" (34.2 × 49.5cm). M. and M. Karolik Collection of American Paintings, 1815–1865, Courtesy of Museum of Fine Arts, Boston. Page 5: William J. Glackens, 1870–1938, *The Captain's Pier*, 1913. Oil on canvas, 26" × 32" (66 × 81.2cm). Private collection/Art Resource, New York.

For my father

Introduction

Sea of stretch'd ground-swells,
Sea breathing broad and convulsive breaths,
Sea of the brine of life and of unshovell'd yet always ready graves,
Howler and scooper of storms, capricious and dainty sea,
I am integral with you, I too am one phase and of all phases.

—Walt Whitman, "Song of Myself," 1881

Few are the forces in nature that can compete with the prodigious awe inspired by the seas. There is little else on our planet that has commanded such fear and respect, for the sea has been deified, immortalized, blessed, and cursed. Water is one of the four cosmic elements that, along with earth, wind, and fire, rules the signs of the zodiac in the ancient science of astrology. Throughout recorded history, the sea has manifested its presence, provoking wonder and necessitating invention to explain its origins. Virtually every culture has its creation myth, or divinities of the "first time." For the Egyptians it was Nun, or chaos, who embodied the primordial sludge of waters in which all life was immanent. The Chinese believed that the oceans were ruled by five immortals, the sea-dragon kings, who lived in elaborate underwater castles made of colored stones and crystals. It was Poseidon with his trident scepter who ruled the waters in ancient Greek mythology, while most of the Native American tribes of North America believe that a primeval water covered the not-yet-created earth, and that a hero, animal, or human dived into its depths to bring forth some mud from which dry land was then formed. The familiar words of the Old Testament from Genesis 1 read: "In the beginning, when God created the heavens and the earth, the earth was a formless wasteland, and darkness covered the abyss, while a mighty wind swept over the waters." From water comes life, for without it we would die. Most of the water on our planet is found in the vast oceans, which cover 70 percent of the earth's surface.

Of course, geography is the main factor that designates whether it is the sea or another body of water that will appear in a given culture's imagery. Some early examples of sea images in Western art can be found in what were the exquisite murals that adorned the walls of the Queen's Megaron, Palace of Minos, at Knossos, Crete (c. 1600–1400 B.C.), which show finely painted dolphins and fish swimming in turquoise-streaked waters. From about 1500 B.C. is another fresco from a house on what was the island of Thera: the "Flotilla fresco" is an elaborate seascape and landscape scene, which documents in great detail a fleet of ships between two ports, complete with sailors, rowers, and passengers. In the Etruscan Tomb of Hunting and Fishing in Tarquinia, Italy (c. 520 B.C.), an entire room is covered with a great marine panorama that depicts a continuous expanse of water and sky in which fishermen in boats and a hunter equipped with a slingshot try their skill in capturing a frenzy of flying birds and leaping fish. The Romans were famous for their house decoration, covering interior walls with a range of scenes, a famous example of which are the Odyssey Landscapes, dating from the late first century B.C. *Laestrygonians Hurling Rocks at the Fleet of Odysseus* illustrates a story from the Homer epic in which Odysseus and his men are attacked by giants perched precariously on large rocks jutting from the sea.

With the advent of Christianity came a noticeable diminution in the artistic representation of things that were deemed pagan and frivolous. Biblical stories replaced the earlier myths, and the promise of spiritual reward was emphasized through church mosaics and manuscript illuminations. Scenes such as *The Crossing of the Red Sea*, *Noah and the Ark*, *The Baptism of Christ*, and *Jonah Being Swallowed by the Whale* had instructional as well as aesthetic value. At the time, the people of medieval Europe had somewhat of an aversion to water and were not inclined to bathe frequently, because of the belief that the bubonic plague and other fatal diseases could be spread by doing so. It follows, then, that the closest allusion to a "seascape" in the Middle Ages would perhaps be a work such as *Sawfish Flying Over a Boat* (c. 1185), an illuminated manuscript page in a bestiary. Prompted by an ever-increasing interest in the physical world, bestiaries were volumes that combined descriptions of both real and imaginary creatures with moralizing allegories. *Sawfish Flying Over a Boat* shows an enormous sawfish jumping over two sailors, much to their amazement, in a boat at sea.

It wasn't until the middle years of the Italian Renaissance that the ocean was represented in a more relaxed manner. Patronage of the arts by wealthy Italian families who commissioned architecture and beautiful religious altarpieces, as well as portraiture and works of a more secular nature, allowed artists like Piero della Francesca, Paolo Uccello, Sandro Botticelli, and Leonardo da Vinci (to name but a few) to produce works of unparalleled excellence. Evidence of this is Botticelli's timeless *The Birth of Venus* (c. 1480).

Simultaneous to the Italian reawakening of art was the development of a different but no less important aesthetic in northern Europe. Pieter Brueghel the Elder, a late Northern Renaissance master, was one of Holland's most accomplished and prolific painters. Known for his peasant scenes as well as his Boschian canvases of biting satire, he chronicled Dutch country life of the sixteenth century. It follows that his *Fall of Icarus* (c. 1554–1558) emphasizes the bucolic scenery and the sailing ship on the water beyond, and makes only a slight allusion to the myth of Icarus. By the seventeenth century, though, maritime scenes were most important in the Netherlands, and the work of artists such as Willem van de Velde the Younger was very much in demand. Van de Velde's naval portraits and numerous depictions of the sea, particularly his "calms" like *Pier: A Calm (Dutch Vessels Close Inshore at Low Tide and Men Bathing)* (1661), mark a definite recognition of the seascape genre. More scenes of the beach and the people who gathered there to work and play would come later in the century, further distinguishing Dutch seascapes from formal maritime painting.

In France, however, emphasis on the representation of bustling seaports was predominant. Claude Lorrain brought this genre to fantastic heights in the seventeenth century by painting imagined harbor scenes like *The Debarkation of Cleopatra at Tarsus,* where everything but the sea and sky was elaborately fabricated. Claude-Joseph Vernet continued, albeit more truthfully, this tradition of marine painting into the eighteenth century, when he was commissioned by King Louis XV to produce a series of twenty-six paintings of French ports (two per port), twelve of which he completed between 1753 and 1762. He painted the works on-site, and became known as one of the preeminent maritime artists of his day.

The Romantic movement of the early nineteenth century was epitomized by an artistic call to arms in a "return to nature." What better vehicle for the expression of this philosophy than the glorification of the land and sea? Whether through the eyes of an early advocate like American Washington Allston or from the more mature vision of German artist Caspar David Friedrich, the Romanticists raised seascape painting to a new level of appreciation. By the end of the century, coastal resorts in Europe had gained popularity among the upper classes, and French artist Eugène-Louis Boudin's paintings, which portrayed those very people in casual congregation by the sea, were sought after eagerly. Boudin also documented the seaside resort of Trouville, where he worked alongside French Impressionist Claude Monet. The school of French Impressionism, with its plein air (out-of-doors) theories of painting, had far-reaching effects in terms of how artists would see the world. Older, established painters, like Édouard Manet and Edgar Degas, didn't completely succumb to the influence of the movement, but they did occasionally experiment. The work of British

Impressionists, such as Walter Richard Sickert and Philip Wilson Steer, has a markedly different feeling, which may be due in part to the urban environment in which most of their paintings are set; however, even their beach scenes are stylistically distinct from other practitioners of the Impressionist principles. The staccato brush strokes employed by Steer in *Sands of Boulogne* (1892) create a sense of strong and highly reflective light that bounces off his figures and the landscape in a charged and vivacious manner. Spaniard Joaquín Sorolla y Bastida and Scandinavian Peder Severin Krøyer each captured the distinct light and atmospheric effects of their respective countries in their paintings, and created unique and luminous depictions of their beaches and waters in the Impressionist tradition.

The twentieth century brought an entirely new set of concepts and metaphors to the subject at hand, reflective of the dramatic changes in sociological temperament and the result of vast technological progress worldwide. In America a revolt against the traditional and staid academic school of thinking provoked a trend toward Realism that was manifest in the work of New York–based artists like John Sloan, George Wesley Bellows, and Edward Hopper. At one time, these artists had all studied with the influential painter Robert Henri, a member of "the Eight," who had encouraged them to find inspiration from their surroundings. In *South Beach Bathers* (1907–1908), John Sloan focuses on the interaction of the people at the scene rather than on the beauty of the environment; he conveys a sense of their mood and attitudes through their various gestures and expressions. The art of both George Wesley Bellows and Edward Hopper is also more commonly associated with representations of urban life, but there is a pleasant departure from the cityscape. Bellows spent a lot of time painting the rustic coastal scenery of Maine, where he produced some of his most brilliant work. *The Big Dory* (1913) reverberates with bright, bold colors in an exuberant celebration of a typical northeastern scene, the launching of a boat into water by hardworking fishermen. *Jo Sketching at the Beach* (1923–1924) by Edward Hopper is a quiet and intimate painting of the artist's wife absorbed in her own work. The use of watercolor is particularly appropriate, giving this beautiful study a feeling of lightness and spontaneity.

Another group of artists that incited a spirit of change in the direction of abstract painting called their style Precisionism, a movement that was inspired by science and the modern. Georgia O'Keeffe and Charles Sheeler were just two among a group of numerous painters, photographers, and writers who depicted industrial America in a ideological idealization of beauty. Sheeler's magnificent work *Pertaining to Yachts and Yachting* (1922) exemplifies the Precisionist approach to this nearly abstract style in a clean, "precise" fashion. Likewise, O'Keeffe employs characteristic simplicity of form and rich color to evoke the feeling of ocean waves crashing on a dark, empty beach in her captivating seascape *Wave, Night* (1928).

By the middle of the twentieth century, art exploded onto a forceful new path in the form of Abstract Expressionism. Jackson Pollock embodied this shocking break with representational painting via his rhythmic action paintings. He perhaps best summed up the new attitude toward making art when he said, "It doesn't make much difference how the paint is put on as long as something has been said. Technique is just a means at arriving at a statement." In *Blue (Moby Dick)* (c. 1943), Pollock interprets the seascape by means of another type of abstraction reminiscent of the work of Joan Miró. The pervasive use of the color blue filled with quirky expressive shapes makes it possible to imagine a turbulent sea alive with writhing life-forms. And Milton Avery's *Dunes and Sea II* (1960), a spiritual, tranquil observation of the sea's natural beauty, needs no verbal elaboration or translation to explain why he is considered one of the finest artists of the twentieth century. The image of the sea is timeless and will continue to be recorded so long as there are artists and art lovers who will seek out its enigmatic and therapeutic presence.

Pieter Brueghel the Elder

Fall of Icarus

c. 1554–1558

Tempera and oil on canvas, 29" × 44" (73.6 × 111.7cm). Musées Royaux des Beaux-Arts de Belgique, Brussels.

Fall of Icarus illustrates the Greek myth of Daedalus and Icarus. At the request of Queen Pasiphaë of Crete, Daedalus, craftsman and inventor, built a wooden cow in which the queen could meet her lover, a sacred bull. Afterward, Daedalus built the Labryinth to hide the offspring of their ill-fated union, the Minotaur, a monster part human and part bull. Furious at Daedalus for helping his wife, King Minos banished the inventor and his son, Icarus, to the maze. As Daedalus and Icarus prepared their escape on wings fashioned from wax and feathers, Daedalus counseled his son not to fly too close to the water and the sun. But in his excitement, Icarus forgot his father's warning; he flew higher and higher, melted his wings, and plunged to his death in the Aegean Sea. Pieter Brueghel the Elder's (c. 1525–1569) painting shows a plowman, a shepherd, and a fisherman—all going about their daily business, seemingly unaware of the hapless Icarus, whose legs can be seen disappearing into the depths of the water at the lower right portion of the canvas, thus making reference to an old German proverb which suggests that "no plow comes to a standstill because a man dies." This scene also demonstrates Brueghel's moralizing tendency, a quality that frequently invites comparison of his work to that of Hieronymus Bosch, another Dutch master.

WILLEM VAN DE VELDE THE YOUNGER

Pier: A Calm (Dutch Vessels Close Inshore at Low Tide and Men Bathing)

1661

OIL ON CANVAS, 24⅞" × 28⅜" (63.2 × 72CM). NATIONAL GALLERY, LONDON.

Willem van de Velde the Younger (1633–1707) was born into a family of painters. An accomplished artist in his own right, he is best known for his close alliance with his father, the famous ship portraitist Willem van de Velde the Elder, whose younger son, Adriaen, achieved his reputation separately as a landscape artist. Based in Amsterdam, Willem the Elder often traveled as an independent observer on ships at sea, carefully sketching a great variety of sailing vessels and their maneuvers; his drawings then served as reference for Willem the Younger's paintings. Maritime painting was in great demand in seventeenth-century Holland, and Willem the Younger depicted the sea in every state imaginable: he painted sea battles, storms, ship portraits, naval maneuvers, and royal embarkations. This "calm" was one of his many studies of the sea at rest, which might have served as a metaphor for humankind's livelihood or harmonious relationship with God and nature. In the early 1670s, the French invasion of Holland prompted the van de Velde family to leave their country for England, where they were appointed to the court of King Charles II and lived out their lives in royal service as marine artists.

Claude-Joseph Vernet

Night: Seaport with Moonlight Effect

1773

Oil on canvas, $38\frac{10}{16}$" × $64\frac{15}{16}$" (98.1 × 164.9cm). Musée du Louvre, Paris.

Night: Seaport with Moonlight Effect by Claude-Joseph Vernet (1714–1789) is one of a set of four paintings representing the different times of day—early morning, midday, late afternoon, and night—that were commissioned in 1773 by the Countess du Barry for the Pavillon de Louveciennes. Born in Avignon, Vernet first studied with his father, a decorative painter of modest success, then went to live and study in Rome. The story of how he came to be an avowed seascape painter is suitably romantic. It is said that he was so overwhelmed by the magnificent vista of the Mediterranean Sea, which he witnessed en route to Rome, that he jumped from the carriage in which he was riding and proclaimed his calling as a marine artist. Following in the Claudian tradition of the Romantic Neoclassical seascapes, the theme of man in nature—bearing witness to violent storms and beautiful sunsets, by moonlight and in early morning calm—served to animate an entire world of sailors, fishermen, merchants, laundresses, and bathers for Vernet, and was a subject to which he often returned during his long and successful career.

WASHINGTON ALLSTON

Coast Scene on the Mediterrean

1811

OIL ON CANVAS, 34" × 40" (86.4 × 101.6CM). COLUMBIA MUSEUM OF ART, SOUTH CAROLINA.

Washington Allston (1779–1843), an American landscape and history painter, represents a link between American and European Romantic art—particularly in England, where he befriended many artists, poets, and intellectuals of like-minded philosophy. Allston's artistic sensibility was formed in New England, but it was in Europe that he developed the technique, training, and subject matter that enabled him to express his metaphysical ideals. He traveled to Rome and London, where he first achieved success on a large scale, between 1811 and 1818. *Coast Scene on the Mediterranean* was painted three years after Allston had last seen the Mediterranean, but he believed that past scenes are "in effect the truest, so long as through the mysterious memory they can give that thrilling play of life which present realities deny." In this painting, Allston illustrates his belief that harmony—between mind and spirit, man and nature—is the central principle of the universe. He achieves this by literally painting the rays of the setting sun with reverberating values of physical color. The radiating light of violet, blue, and gold begins and ends at the composition's focal point, uniting the figures in the foreground with the vast expanse of water and sky.

CASPAR DAVID FRIEDRICH

Moonrise by the Sea

1822

OIL ON CANVAS, 21⅝" × 28" (55 × 71CM). PREUSSISCHER KULTURBESITZ, NATIONALGALERIE, STAATLICHE MUSEEN ZU BERLIN.

Caspar David Friedrich's (1774–1840) *Moonrise by the Sea* was created as a companion piece to a painting entitled *The Solitary Tree (Village Landscape in Morning Light).* The two canvases were intended to be viewed together, but *Moonrise* is a work of serene beauty on its own. The three figures dressed in city clothes in the center of the canvas face out toward the Baltic Sea. Perched on a large group of rocks, they gather in silence to watch nature's spectacle. Everything about the composition suggests contemplation and peace—the clouds open up to show the sphere of the ascending moon, creating an upward curve of light that is echoed in the opposite direction by the rounded earthbound solidity of the rocks, thus balancing heaven and earth. The gentle movement of the water can be discerned by the shimmering moonlight playing on its surface. This painting sends a out a message of hope through the communal experience of the seated trio, and their youthful expectations for the future can be shared as they look out toward the incoming ships returning from remote and mysterious places.

William Dyce

Pegwell Bay: A Recollection of October 5th, 1858

c. 1858–1860

Oil on canvas, 25" × 35" (63.5 × 88.9cm). Tate Gallery, London.

Pegwell Bay: A Recollection of October 5th, 1858 by William Dyce (1806–1864) is essentially a family portrait. The man carrying a paint box at the mid-distance on the far right is Dyce himself. In the foreground are, from right to left, his wife, Jane; Jane's sisters, Grace and Isabella; and one of Dyce's sons. Together they are collecting seashells at low tide; yet despite their pleasant task, the overall mood of the scene is somber. The figures seem isolated, absorbed in their own thoughts—notice how mother and son are looking off to the left at something beyond the canvas. The simultaneous small scale and sharp focus of the figures distances them from each other and the viewer psychologically. In fact, the figures seem trapped in time, encapsulated as in a snapshot. That Dyce was an amateur scientist can clearly be seen here in both his precise rendering of the distant chalk cliffs and the atmospheric light conditions of the autumn afternoon. There is an interesting detail in the picture: a barely discernible light streak at the uppermost center of the work. The streak is Donati's comet, first witnessed by Giovanni Battista Donati at Florence on June 2, 1858.

JAMES ABBOTT MCNEILL WHISTLER

Crepuscule in Flesh Colour and Green: Valparaiso

1866

OIL ON CANVAS, 23" × 29⅞" (58.4 × 75.8CM). TATE GALLERY, LONDON.

American artist James Abbott McNeill Whistler (1834–1903) spent most of his adult life living in London. He made an indelible impression with his large walrus mustache and trademark monocle, and his rather eccentric ways gained him notoriety in the art world. Stylistically, Whistler falls somewhere in between the decorativeness of the Pre-Raphaelites and the light-filled art of French Impressionism. He set himself apart from other artists of his time by focusing on the pure aesthetics of atmosphere. To this effect, he chose to give his pictures musical names, like "arrangements" and "nocturnes." In 1866, Whistler was asked to join in a war effort, which he flippantly described as "a moment when many of the adventurers the [American Civil] War had made of many Southerners were knocking about London, hunting for something to do, and, I hardly know how, but the something resolved itself into an expedition to go out to help the Chileans…against the Spaniards." This painting shows the harbor of Valparaiso, Chile, at sunset. Filled with warships readying for departure, the scene is deceptively calm, for this work most likely represents the evening before the bombardment of March 31, 1866, when the French fleet left the town and its residents to the mercy of the Spanish.

WINSLOW HOMER

On the Beach

1870

OIL ON CANVAS, 16" × 25" (40.6 × 63.5CM).
COLLECTION OF CANAJOHARIE LIBRARY AND ART GALLERY, CANAJOHARIE, NEW YORK.

Winslow Homer (1836–1910) was virtually self-taught. Born in Boston, he received his only artistic training during a two-year apprenticeship to lithographer John H. Bufford. Afterward, when he was only twenty-one years old, Homer took a studio of his own and embarked on a career as a freelance illustrator. Homer moved to New York in 1859, about the time of his emergence as a painter. He is most noted for his scenes of the American Civil War, country life, and dramatic seascapes. He was never particularly social and became more reclusive as he aged. He moved to Prout's Neck, Maine, at the peak of his fame in the 1880s and lived there until his death. *On the Beach* was originally part of a larger painting, *On the Beach, Long Branch*, a then-popular New Jersey beach resort. What remains is the center portion of the cut-down canvas. The initial composition was symmetrical, with a group of bathers on the right-hand side of the painting. To date, two of the three portions have been located.

Elihu Vedder

Memory

1870

Oil on mahogany panel, 20$\frac{5}{16}$" × 14$\frac{3}{4}$" (51.5 × 37.4cm).
Mr. and Mrs. William Preston Harrison Collection, Los Angeles County Museum of Art.

Elihu Vedder (1836–1923) was an American painter who, although born in New York, spent the majority of his life in Rome, Italy. In this work, he marries the evocative presence of the sea with a personal vision. At first glance, *Memory* appears to be nothing more than a painting of a dark stormy sky over a barren coast. But upon closer inspection, one can see the face of a woman in the clouds; the woman is Carrie Vedder, the artist's wife, whom he married in 1869. It is believed that *Memory* was based on a drawing he made on Carrie's birthday, March 19, in 1867. The combination of a realistic seascape with a sentimental, ghostly apparition is typical of Vedder's Symbolist style—his allusions to the power of the unconscious mind. Ahead of his time, Vedder anticipated the Surrealist movement of the early twentieth century.

Édouard Manet

On the Beach

1873

Oil on canvas, 23½" × 28⅞" (59.6 × 73.2cm). Musée d'Orsay, Paris.

Édouard Manet (1832–1883) painted this charming portrait of his wife, Suzanne, who is shown reading, her face protected from wind and sand by a veil tied over her hat, and his brother, Eugène, in the summer of 1873 during a stay with his family at Berck-sur-Mer, France. Although *On the Beach* is in essence a simple rendering of an afternoon by the sea, the composition of the canvas is very effective. The two figures are seated together at an oblique angle; their bodies turned away from the viewer, they face out toward the water. By placing the figures up against the picture plane, Manet creates a sense of inclusion and intimacy, as if the viewer might be standing right behind them. It is almost certain that Manet painted *On the Beach* from life, which is in keeping with the French Impressionist tradition of painting in plein air, or out-of-doors, as there is sand in the paint.

Edgar Degas

At the Seaside

c. 1876

Oil on paper mounted on canvas, 18½" × 32½" (47 × 82.5cm). National Gallery, London.

At the Seaside by Edgar Degas (1834–1917) was first shown in 1877 in Paris at the third Impressionist Exhibition. The subject of the painting, a seascape, is almost unique within Degas' body of work and was developed in full consciousness of the seascape scenes of his colleagues Boudin, Manet, and Monet, while it also alluded to photographs of seaside bathers, which were fairly common at the time. Degas was known to use photographs regularly as reference for his paintings and to produce exhaustive preparatory drawings. Unlike most of the French Impressionists, he chose to paint in his studio using models and photographs rather than life in "nature." He preferred to be called a "Realist" and, to further distinguish himself from the Impressionists' main concern with color and atmosphere, concentrated on portraying the human form (as opposed to landscapes). In doing so, he created a representation of contemporary life. Accordingly, the central focus of *At the Seaside* are the figures of the little girl lying under an umbrella and her nanny, who is combing the child's hair. The naturalistic poses of the two figures, along with the obviously nurturing gesture of grooming, conveys a sense of familiarity and even tenderness between the two.

Pierre-Cécile Puvis de Chavannes

Young Girls at the Edge of the Sea

1879

Oil on canvas, 80$\frac{11}{16}$" × 60$\frac{5}{8}$" (205 × 154cm). Musée d'Orsay, Paris.

"As for the greatest artist of our time, Puvis de Chavannes [1824–1898], did he not try his best to spread all around us that sweet serenity to which we all aspire? His sublime landscapes, where Holy Nature seems to cradle upon her bosom a humanity at once loving, wise, noble, and simple, surely provide us with an admirable lesson. He has expressed everything, this incomparable genius—help for the weak, love of work, self-sacrifice, respect for high thought. It sheds a wonderful light upon our era. It is sufficient to look at one of his masterpieces...to feel capable of noble deeds." This eulogistic quote by sculptor Auguste Rodin in 1911 attests to the great respect Puvis de Chavannes was accorded by his fellow artists. Known for his friezelike murals painted in a delicate palette of subdued color, Puvis de Chavannes influenced many early modern painters with his monumental compositions. *Young Girls at the Edge of the Sea* is a subtle study of rhythm and asymmetrical balance. The curved mound of sand flows continuously into the undulating forms of the reclining women. The empty sea stands as a counterpoint to them both and intersects the standing figure centrally, like a cross.

P. Puvis de Chavannes

PEDER SEVERIN KRØYER

Fishermen on the Skagen Beach

1883

OIL ON CANVAS, 58" × 80¼" (147.3 × 203.8CM). STATENS MUSEUM FOR KUNST, COPENHAGEN.

At the northernmost tip of Denmark, where the Kagerak and the Kattegat seas meet, is the Cape of Skagen, or the Skaw. Here, at the turn of the twentieth century, a community of Scandinavian artists assembled who, having trained in Paris, were applying the principles of Impressionism to portray their unique Nordic landscape and lifestyle. Peder Severin Krøyer (1851–1909) was born in Norway but grew up in Denmark. After studying at the Royal Academy of Art in Copenhagen, he traveled throughout Europe, stopping to work in Paris from 1877 to 1879, and continued his travels until 1882, when he met Danish painters Michael and Anna Ancher at the World Exposition in Vienna. The couple invited him to visit Skagen, where Anna's father owned a hotel. Krøyer arrived in July of that year; the Skaw ultimately became his second home. *Fishermen on the Skagen Beach,* one of Krøyer's early works, captures a characteristic Nordic climactic condition called *stemning,* or the "blue-hour," a result of the lingering effects of twilight on the long midsummer evenings. Here, Krøyer is asserting the effects of Impressionism, or Luminism, in an attempt to create the illusion of forms bathed in the light and atmosphere particular to Scandinavia. The misty blue haze that pervades the scene and blankets the prostrate figures of the fishermen attests to the evocative power of Luminist art.

GEORGES-PIERRE SEURAT

The Lighthouse at Honfleur

1886

OIL ON CANVAS, 26¼" × 32¼" (66.7 × 81.9CM).
COLLECTION OF MR. AND MRS. PAUL MELLON, NATIONAL GALLERY OF ART, WASHINGTON, D.C.

Georges-Pierre Seurat (1859–1891) is most associated with Pointillism, his technique of painting in small dabs of divided color. Seurat and his followers claimed that they could capture the illusion of prismatic light scientifically. His dotted brushwork set him apart from the French Impressionists and was dubbed "Neo-Impressionism" by the critics. Moreover, his paintings shocked the public, who couldn't make sense of the new visual effects created by Seurat's method of painting, referred to as Divisionism. At the top of his palette, Seurat would place a line of primary colors; at the bottom, a row of white dabs. Between the two rows he would create a third row of color blended from the two others. From all three lines he would make his dots and strokes of various shapes and colors, all of which would meld together when viewed from a certain distance. *The Lighthouse at Honfleur* is one of a series of seascapes executed between 1886 and 1888. Seurat died prematurely at age thirty-one of a sudden illness. Camille Pissaro, in a letter to his son, wrote: "Yesterday I went to Seurat's funeral.…I believe you are right, Pointillism is finished, but I think it will give rise to other effects which later will have great artistic significance. Seurat really brought something."

PAUL GAUGUIN

The Seaweed Gatherers

1889

OIL ON CANVAS, 38" × 48¼" (96.5 × 122.5CM). FOLKWANG MUSEUM, ESSEN, GERMANY.

In a letter to Vincent van Gogh, Paul Gauguin (1848–1903) wrote, "At the moment, I am working on a painting of women gathering seaweed on the beach. I have pictured them like boxes rising by steps at regular distanced intervals, in blue clothes and black coifs despite the biting cold. The seaweed they are collecting to fertilize their land is ocher, with tawny highlights. The sand is *pink*, not yellow, probably because it is wet, and the sea is a dark color. I see this scene every day and it is like a gust of wind, a sudden awareness of the struggle for life, of sadness, and of our obedience to the harsh laws of nature."

Before his ultimate retreat to the exotic island of Tahiti, where he produced many of his best-known works, Paul Gauguin spent time in the western French province of Brittany, where he was inspired by the land and its people. *The Seaweed Gatherers* is a highly studied composition which conveys a sense of melancholy and agelessness. The workers seem transfixed by their labors, moving in a dreamlike procession. That Gauguin was greatly influenced by Pierre-Cécile Puvis de Chavannes is apparent in the monumental handling of the figures and the sense of myth bestowed upon the scene.

P Gauguin 89

Philip Wilson Steer

Sands of Boulogne

1892

Oil on canvas, 23⅝" × 29⅞" (60 × 75.8cm). Tate Gallery, London.

British Impressionism evolved as a direct reaction against the moralistic conventions and sentimentality of Victorian society and art. James Abbott McNeill Whistler forged the way for the movement, espousing his avant-garde theories and attracting a following of young artists, who then went on to form their own Impressionist clique, the "London Impressionists," as a way of stressing their urban origins. Like his peers, Philip Wilson Steer (1860–1942) painted the London city scene, but he was primarily a landscape painter. His seascapes are perhaps his best-known and most experimental works. *Sands of Boulogne*, set in France, is a characteristic example of Steer's speckled brushwork and brilliant palette. He displayed a preference for pastel-like blues, purples, and pinks, often using pale yellow for highlights—these became his trademark colors. As he said, "Art is the expression of an impression seen through a personality."

Joaquín Sorolla y Bastida

Children on the Sea-shore (The Young Amphibians)

1903

Oil on canvas, 37⅞" × 51⅜" (96.2 × 130.5cm). W.P. Wilstach Collection, Philadelphia Museum of Art.

Joaquín Sorolla y Bastida (1863–1923), born in Valencia, Spain, rose from humble origins to become an internationally acclaimed painter, winning the Grand Prix at the Universal Exhibition in Paris in 1900. He studied in Italy on a scholarship, then traveled to Paris, where he inevitably was exposed to Impressionist plein-air painting.

Sorolla y Bastida was one of the most successful artists to marry the Impressionist technique to the seascape genre. He painted a variey of images of the Valencian seaside, representing everything from children at play in the water to fishermen hard at work. *Children on the Sea-shore (Young Amphibians)* was painted at the peak of Sorolla's artistic maturity. He had long since settled in Madrid and was very family-oriented; as a result, scenes of children at the beach was an often repeated theme in his work. Sorolla's expansive loose brushwork and dazzling bold color express with exceptional skill the feel of the blazing sun, the sand, and the moving water in a vivacious affirmation of life.

John Sloan

South Beach Bathers

1907–1908

Oil on canvas, 26" × 31¾" (65.7 × 81cm). Walker Art Center, Minneapolis, Minnesota.

John Sloan (1871–1951) left school at sixteen to work so that he could help support his family, finding employment as a cashier in a company that dealt in books, cards, and fine prints. He soon taught himself etching and demonstrated enough ability to secure work as a freelance artist. In 1892, he joined the staff of the Philadelphia *Inquirer* and, later on, the Philadelphia *Press*. This was Sloan's introduction to the art world. He met many artists associated with the Pennsylvania Academy like Robert Henri, Everett Shinn, and William Glackers, with whom he became lifelong friends. After taking night classes at the Academy, Sloan started to paint seriously in the late 1890s. In 1904, following the lead of his friends, he and his wife moved to New York, where he started painting street scenes, the subject with which he would be most identified. In fact, Sloan embodied the essence of the New York Realist movement with his prints and paintings of city life. He and seven other artists (who became known collectively as "The Eight") banded together against "the old grannies of art in New York" by challenging the conventions of the New York Academy and mounting their own exhibition. In *South Beach Bathers,* a scene modeled after a Staten Island beach, Sloan turns from the street to the beach without losing his urban focus, as he observes transplanted city dwellers at play.

John Sloan '08

CHILDE HASSAM

Sunset at Sea

1911

OIL ON CANVAS, 34" (86.4CM) SQUARE. ROSE ART MUSEUM, BRANDEIS UNIVERSITY, WALTHAM, MASSACHUSETTS.

Childe Hassam (1859–1935) is America's foremost Impressionist painter—he is the one whose work most faithfully incorporates the spirit of French Impressionism. Hassam, born in Boston, dropped out of school to work for a wood engraver after a fire destroyed the Hassam family's business; soon he was advanced to staff artist. In 1883, Hassam went to Europe, where he studied for three years at the Academie Julien in Paris, and it was there that he was indelibly influenced by the Impressionists. Hassam was a prolific artist who executed a great diversity of themes; his most famous paintings are his urban scenes, particularly depictions of rainy days, and his flag paintings from World War I. *Sunset at Sea* exhibits the influence of the Post-Impressionistic technique of Divisionism. This painting nears abstraction in the decorative handling and patterning of the water. The composition consists of horizontal bands of broken color, the water being mostly yellow and green, the sky a combination of blue, red, and yellow. The sole visual clue to the subject matter of the painting is the small ship on the distant horizon.

George Wesley Bellows

The Big Dory

1913

Oil on panel, 18" × 22" (45.7 × 55.9cm). New Britain Museum of American Art, New Britain, Connecticut.

When George Wesley Bellows (1882–1925) arrived in New York in 1902, he was determined to be a painter. He studied with Robert Henri, a member of "The Eight." Under Henri's guidance, Bellows painted New York City street scenes and in 1908 exhibited a painting at the National Academy of Design. In that same show hung a painting by Winslow Homer, an artist whose work Bellows greatly admired. Critics were soon commenting on the similarities between the two artists—a writer for the *New York Times* wrote that Homer's painting had "force and freshness driven home in an unexpectedly exhilarating fashion"; likewise, he found a "rugged and almost startling reality" in Bellows' painting. In 1910, Bellows married, and spent his honeymoon in Montauk, Long Island, where he began to paint seascapes. *The Big Dory,* painted three years later on Monhegan Island, Maine, is composed of strong diagonal and horizontal lines, dramatically punctuated by bold color and broad brush strokes.

HELEN MCNICOLL

Under the Shadow of the Tent

1914

OIL ON CANVAS, 32" × 40" (81.3 × 101.6CM). MONTREAL MUSEUM OF FINE ARTS.

Little has been written about Helen McNicoll (1879–1915), a Canadian artist born in Toronto and raised in Montreal. She took classes at the local art association, and her education might have ended there as she was deaf (a result of scarlet fever as a child), which limited her acceptance and possible advancement in society at the time. Displaying artistic talent and interest, she expressed a desire to study abroad, and she enrolled in classes given by artist Algernon Talmage at St. Ives in Cornwall, England, in 1905. There she met English painter Dorothea Sharp, with whom she would develop a strong alliance; the two painted and traveled together until McNicoll's untimely death at thirty-six. McNicoll adhered to the tenets of French Impressionism, concentrating on the study of plein air light and colors. In *Under the Shadow of the Tent*, she portrays an afternoon of genteel recreation, focusing on the play of sunlight and shadow in a carefully constructed composition. She limits her colors to shades of yellow, ocher, and blue, and her brushwork is smooth yet expressive. *Under the Shadow of the Tent* was painted the year before her death, and stands as a tribute to her considerable artistic ability and yet unrealized potential.

Pablo Picasso

The Bathers

1918

Oil on canvas, 27" × 22" (68.6 × 55.9cm). Musée Picasso, Paris.

Pablo Picasso (1881–1973) is perhaps the most famous artist of the twentieth century and certainly one of the most talented and productive painters of all time, starting at the prodigal age of fourteen and working until his death at ninety-one. A painter, sculptor, and poet, he illustrated magazines and designed costumes, stage sets, and ceramics. Endlessly creative, he worked in many styles. Often called the father of Cubism (1907–1916), Picasso's work constantly evolved, reflecting his personal life and the ever-changing world. In 1917 he married his first wife, a Russian ballet dancer. The couple's travels to southern France provided Picasso with new themes—sunbathers, water sports, and nudes by the sea—all of which proved to be a natural extension of his recent studies of dancers at the Ballets Rousses. This period prompted him to analyze the female figure in depth, studying its movement, attitudes, and opportunity for transformation. *The Bathers* was painted in the summer of 1918 at Biarritz. Exemplifying his Neoclassical period (1917–1925), the painting is quite a departure from the geometric and abstract forms of Cubism that predated it.

Charles Sheeler

Pertaining to Yachts and Yachting

1922

Oil on canvas, 20" × 24" (50.8 × 61cm). Philadelphia Museum of Art.

In the early 1920s, Paul Strand wrote to Alfred Steiglitz, fellow photographer and gallery director, about some new films he hoped to make with artist Charles Sheeler (1883–1965). Strand and Sheeler had collaborated together on an prior film entitled *Manhatta*. Their new film subject was the New York Yacht Club, and although the project was never realized, Sheeler became interested in yachts, and produced several drawings and paintings of them. Sheeler, along with artists such as Georgia O'Keeffe, Charles Demuth, and Louis Lozowick, worked in a Cubist-influenced aesthetic that celebrated the modernization of society. These artists found beauty in the workings of machines and industry. Through all artistic mediums—painting, drawing, photography, and film—this movement, Precisionism, found expression. *Pertaining to Yachts and Yachting* is one of Sheeler's finest works. The painting strikes a balance between Precisionism's exactitude and pure abstraction. By repeating fragmented forms, Sheeler's picture conveys a feeling of sequence and motion, making it seem as if there were many yachts when there are just two. Here, Sheeler has found the perfect vehicle for his immaculate and sleek style of painting.

EDWARD HOPPER

Jo Sketching at the Beach

1923–1924

WATERCOLOR ON PAPER, 13⅞" × 20" (35.3 × 50.8CM). WHITNEY MUSEUM OF AMERICAN ART, NEW YORK.

Edward Hopper (1882–1967) studied under Robert Henri, an artist who trained many painters of formidable talent such as George Wesley Bellows and John Sloan. From the beginning of his artistic career, Hopper was drawn to the subject matter that his work now defines: the visual character of twentieth-century America. While many in the Henri group were painting the urban scene, Hopper managed to convey something of its soul. Throughout his life as an artist he painted a vast portrait of America—its railroads, lighthouses, empty streets, mansions, and city apartments—imbuing them all with a peculiar sense of melancholy beauty. With or without human presence, his canvases convey a poignant quality of loneliness in a realistic and impartial manner. In 1924 he married another student of Henri, Josephine Nivison. The two were inseparable, living and working together until Hopper's death. *Jo Sketching at the Beach* is one of many studies Hopper did of his wife; in fact, she modeled for nearly all the female figures in his paintings.

Georgia O'Keeffe

Wave, Night

1928

Oil on canvas, 30" × 36" (76.2 × 91.5cm). Addison Gallery of American Art, Phillips Academy, Andover, Massachusetts.

Georgia O'Keeffe (1887–1986) recollected the spring of 1920 when she visited a friend at York Beach, Maine: "I spent much time walking on the long, lean, sandy beach—often picking up extraordinary things that I kept in large platters of water to paint. When walking I seldom met anyone as it was very early springtime and cold. I loved running down the boardwalk to the ocean—watching the waves come in, spreading over the hard wet beach—the lighthouse steadily bright far over the waves in the evening when it was almost dark. This was one of the great events of the day." O'Keeffe's painting *Wave, Night* is based on that memory. Famous for her paintings of richly modeled forms, she portrayed everything from pure abstractions of shape to architecture to objects found in the natural world, such as trees, clouds, flowers, and stones. She immortalized America's southwestern landscape of hills, adobe churches, and sun-bleached bones—themes with which she would become identified forever. O'Keeffe simplifed her compositions to the barest minimum, often enlarging and reducing her subjects to clean, intensely colored shapes and patterns, as is evident in *Wave, Night*, where the water and sky merge in a velvety union and where the dot that is the lighthouse is barely distinguishable in the darkness.

ABRAHAM WALKOWITZ

Bathers on the Rocks

c. 1930–1935

OIL ON CANVAS, 25" × 30⅛" (63.5 × 76.2CM). TAMPA MUSEUM OF ART.

Abraham Walkowitz (1878–1965) studied in Europe from 1906 to 1909. The time he spent in France was significant: he arrived right after the Fauve Exhibition of 1905, which heralded the emergence of important artists like Matisse, Derain, and Vlamnick. (Fauvism was a Post-Impressionist movement characterized by vivid antinaturalistic color and distorted composition used as a means to a new expressive end.) Through his art school classmate, Max Weber, he met Leo and Gertrude Stein, the famous patrons and champions of modern art and literature. When he returned to New York, Walkowitz exhibited his work at Alfred Steiglitz's "291" gallery, where he later organized several exhibitions of children's art, as he admired its simplicity and spontaneity. Walkowitz worked in the Fauve manner, flattening space and form, using bright, aggressive colors and heavy outlines. This is evident in his *Bathers on the Rocks*, where the scene is presented from a bird's-eye view, reducing the subject to a cluster of patterned shapes and colors, and creating a rhythmic compositional style. *Bathers on the Rocks* is a work which throbs with movement and visual play in the careful arrangement of forms. According to Walkowitz: "Art is creation and not imitation. Art has its own life."

A. WALKOWITZ

Reginald Marsh

Negroes on Rockaway Beach

1934

Egg tempera on composition board, 30" × 40" (76.2 × 101.6cm). Whitney Museum of American Art, New York.

Reginald Marsh (1898–1954), the son of two artists, began to draw at an early age. Upon graduation from Yale University, he moved to New York and worked as a freelance illustrator and caricaturist for several newspapers and magazines. In 1923, he joined the Whitney Studio Club, precursor of the Whitney Museum of American Art in New York; it was there he had his first one-man exhibition. Never without a sketchbook, Marsh took to recording the drama of the streets, which, during the Great Depression, was exalted to a frenzied crescendo. Among his favorite haunts were Fourteenth Street, where he had his studio; the Bowery; and the local beaches. Drawn to the sea of human anatomy, he produced countless studies of Coney Island. *Negroes on Rockaway Beach* is one of his many excessively busy seascapes where the people provide the subject and the scenery. In Marsh's characteristic fashion, the composition is tightly pressed up against the picture plane, which places the observer smack in the midst of the sunbathers' free-for-all activity. In this painting, however, Marsh leaves open a path, almost as an invitation to join the scene.

DAILY MIRROR
BRIDE QUITS ASTOR
IN STREET QUARRE

PHILIP EVERGOOD

Love on the Beach

1937

OIL ON CANVAS, 30¼" × 37½" (77.5 × 95.3CM). HUNTER GALLERY OF ART, CHATTANOOGA, TENNESSEE.

The art of Philip Evergood (1901–1975) defies categorization. Born in New York but educated in England, Evergood followed a tortuous path to develop his artistic expression. At the Art Students League in New York, he briefly studied under George Luks, one of the original "Eight," whose paintings of urban life influenced him greatly. But it wasn't until the 1930s that Evergood defined his individual approach to art. He painted for the Public Works of Art Project and the Works Progress Administration (a result of the New Deal) in the Social Realist tradition of artists like Ben Shahn. As he matured, Evergood abandoned his propagandist themes of social concern for more personal subject matter—his friends, family, and surroundings—cultivating a unique style which blended accurate observation with fantasy bordering on the surreal. Evergood is at his most playful in *Love on the Beach,* a scene that could have been painted as easily from life as from his prolific imagination. The three couples are entwined in joyful abandon by the sea, dancing and happily absorbed with one another. Even the crabs seem to be joining in on their fun. Evergood's sketchy use of outline and bright color accentuates the mood of lively mirth in this painting.

Philip Evergood

Jackson Pollock

Blue (Moby Dick)

c. 1943

Gouache and ink on composition board, 18¾" × 23⅞" (47.6 × 60.7cm). Ohara Museum of Art, Kurashiki, Japan.

Described by one of his five brothers as being sensitive, easily hurt, inward, and withdrawn, Jackson Pollock's (1912–1956) psychological problems manifested themselves early in his life. As he grew older, these difficulties were compounded by bouts of alcoholism and severe depression. In 1930 Pollock left high school in Wyoming for New York City. There he studied with Thomas Hart Benton at the Art Students League, where he hurled his turbulent energy into his work. From Benton he received a formal training, but it was Pollock's involvement with Jungian therapy that released his creativity and instilled in him the belief that painting sprang from the unconscious. He experimented with many different painting styles but became most famous for his "action" paintings, which he made by literally pouring, dribbling, and swirling paint onto a canvas rolled out on his studio floor. Epitomizing the school of Abstract Expressionism, Pollock shattered the conventions of the art world with his explosive technique. *Blue (Moby Dick)* was created prior to Pollock's development of poured paintings. Although the painting is abstract, Pollock alludes to figuration by suggesting choppy waves in the lower half of the canvas and using biomorphic shapes to represent a deep blue sea teeming with marine life.

Milton Avery

Dunes and Sea II

1960

Oil on canvas, 51⅞" × 72" (131.8 × 182.9cm). Whitney Museum of American Art, New York.

Milton Avery's (1885–1965) paintings possess a soothing quality of simplicity that is deceptively facile. Friend and fellow artist Mark Rothko once described Avery as "a great poet. His is the poetry of sheer loveliness, of sheer beauty.... There have been several others in our generation who have celebrated the world around them, but none with that inevitability where the poetry penetrated every pore of the canvas to the very last touch of the brush. For Avery was a great poet-inventor who had invented sonorities never seen nor heard before." Avery devoted himself entirely to art, while his wife supported him and provided an environment free of financial or social responsibilities. His paintings consisted mainly of landscapes and seascapes, as well as the calm manifestations of his personal world—his friends, family, and surroundings—which he portrayed in his vanguard quasi-abstract style. Celebrated as a rare and gifted colorist, Avery painted *Dunes and Sea II* near the end of his life, and it exemplifies his deep response to nature.

Milton Avery 1960

PHOTOGRAPHY CREDITS

Pieter Brueghel the Elder, c. 1525–1569, *Landscape with Fall of Icarus*, c. 1554–1558. Tempera and oil on canvas, 29" × 44" (73.6 × 111.7cm). Musées Royaux des Beaux-Arts de Belgique, Brussels, Belgium/Art Resource, New York

Willem van de Velde the Younger, 1633–1707, *Pier: A Calm (Dutch Vessels Close Inshore at Low Tide and Men Bathing)*, 1661. Oil on canvas, 24⅞" × 28⅜" (63.2 × 72cm). The National Gallery, London/Reproduced Courtesy of the Trustees

Claude-Joseph Vernet, 1714–1789, *Night: Seaport with Moonlight Effect*, 1773. Oil on canvas, 38$\frac{10}{16}$" × 64$\frac{15}{16}$" (98.1 × 164.9cm). Musée du Louvre, Paris/©Photo R.M.N., Paris

Washington Allston, 1779–1843, *Coast Scene on the Mediterrean*, 1811. Oil on canvas, 34" × 40" (86.4 × 101.6cm). 1957.14. Columbia Museum of Art, South Carolina. Gift of Dr. Robert W. Gibbes, III/Signed B.L.: W. Allston

Casper David Friedrich, 1774–1840, *Moonrise by the Sea*, 1822. Oil on canvas, 21⅝" × 28" (55 × 71cm). Preussischer Kulturbesitz, Nationalgalerie, Staatliche Museen zu Berlin/A.K.G., Berlin

William Dyce, 1806–1864, *Pegwell Bay: A Recollection of October 5th, 1858*, c. 1858–1860. Oil on canvas, 25" × 35" (63.5 × 88.9cm). The Tate Gallery, London/Art Resource, New York

James Abbott McNeill Whistler, 1834–1903, *Crepusule in Flesh Colour and Green: Valparaiso*, 1866. Oil on canvas, 23" × 29⅞" (58.4 × 75.8cm). The Tate Gallery, London, Presented by W. Graham Robertson 1940/Art Resource, New York

Winslow Homer, 1836–1910, *On the Beach*, 1870. Oil on canvas, 16" × 25" (40.6 × 63.5cm). Collection of Canajoharie Library and Art Gallery, Canajoharie, New York

Elihu Vedder, 1836–1923, *Memory*, 1870. Oil on mahogany panel, 20$\frac{5}{16}$" × 14¾" (51.5 × 37.4cm). Los Angeles County Museum of Art. Mr. & Mrs. William Preston Harrison Collection, Los Angeles, California

Édouard Manet, 1832–1883, *On the Beach*, 1873. Oil on canvas, 23½" × 28⅞" (59.6 × 73.2cm). Musée d'Orsay, Paris/©Photo R.M.N., Paris

Edgar Degas, 1834–1917, *At the Seaside*, c. 1876. Oil on paper mounted on canvas, 18½" × 32½" (47 × 82.5cm). National Gallery, London. Reproduced Courtesy of the Trustees

Pierre-Cécile Puvis de Chavannes, 1824–1898, *Young Girls at the Edge of the Sea*, 1879. Oil on canvas, 80$\frac{11}{16}$" × 60⅝" (205 × 154cm). Musée d'Orsay, Paris/©Photo R.M.N., Paris

Peder Severin Krøyer, 1851–1909, *Fishermen on the Skagen Beach*, 1883. Oil on canvas, 58" × 80¼" (147.3 × 203.8cm). Statens Museum for Kunst, Copenhagen

Georges-Pierre Seurat, 1859–1891, *The Lighthouse at Honfleur*, 1886. Oil on canvas, 26¼" × 32¼" (66.7 × 81.9cm). National Gallery of Art, Washington, D.C., Collection of Mr. and Mrs. Paul Mellon, ©1995 Board of Trustees

Paul Gauguin, 1848–1903, *The Seaweed Gatherers*, 1889. Oil on canvas, 38" × 48¼" (96.5 × 122.5cm). Folkwang Museum, Essen, Germany

Philip Wilson Steer, 1860–1942, *Sands of Boulogne*, 1892. Oil on canvas, 23⅝" × 29⅞" (60 × 75.8cm). The Tate Gallery, London/Art Resource, New York

Joaquín Sorolla y Bastida, 1863–1923, *The Young Amphibians*, 1903. Oil on canvas, 37⅜" × 51⅜" (96.2 × 130.5cm). Philadelphia Museum of Art, Philadelphia. W.P. Wilstach Fund. Photo by Graydon Wood, 1995

John Sloan, 1871–1951, *South Beach Bathers*, 1907–1908. Oil on canvas, 26" × 31¾" (65.7 × 81cm). Walker Art Center, Minneapolis, Minnesota. Gift of the T.B. Walker Foundation, Gilbert M. Walker Fund, 1948

Childe Hassam, 1859–1935, *Sunset at Sea*, 1911. Oil on canvas, 34" × 34" (86.4 × 86.4cm). Rose Art Museum, Brandeis University, Waltham, Massachusetts, Gift of Mr. and Mrs. Monroe Geller, New York/Photo by Muldoon Studio

George Wesley Bellows, 1882–1925, *The Big Dory*, 1913. Oil on panel, 18" × 22" (45.7 × 55.9cm). New Britain Museum of American Art, New Britain, Connecticut. Harriet R. Stanley Fund/Photo by E. Irving Blomstrann

Helen McNicoll, 1879–1915, *Under the Shadow of the Tent*, 1914. Oil on canvas, 32" × 40" (81.3 × 101.6cm). Collection of the Montreal Museum of Fine Arts, Montreal, 915.122. Gift of Mr. and Mrs. David McNicoll/Photo by Brian Merett, MMFA

Pablo Picasso, 1881–1973, *The Bathers*, 1918. Oil on canvas, 27" × 22" (68.6 × 55.9cm). Musée Picasso, Paris/©Photo R.M.N., Paris

Charles Sheeler, 1883–1965, *Pertaining to Yachts and Yachting*, 1922. Oil on canvas, 20" × 24" (50.8 × 61cm). Philadelphia Museum of Art, Philadelphia. Bequest of Margaretta S. Hinchman

Edward Hopper, 1882–1967, *Jo Sketching at Good Harbor Beach*, 1923–1924. Watercolor on paper, 13⅞" × 20" (35.3 × 50.8cm). Whitney Museum of American Art, New York. Bequest of Josephine N. Hopper. 70.112

Georgia O'Keeffe, 1887–1986, *Wave, Night*, 1928. Oil on canvas, 30" × 36" (76.2 × 91.5cm). 1947.33, Purchased as the gift of Charles L. Stillman (PA 1922) ©Addison Gallery of American Art, Phillips Academy, Andover, Massachusetts. All Rights Reserved

Reginald Marsh, 1898–1954, *Negroes on Rockaway Beach*, 1934. Egg tempera on composition board, 30" × 40" (76.2 × 101.6cm). Whitney Museum of American Art, New York. Gift of Mr. and Mrs. Albert Hackett

Abraham Walkowitz, 1878–1965, *Bathers on the Rocks*, c. 1930–1935. Oil on canvas, 25" × 30⅛" (63.5 × 76.2cm). Collection of Tampa Museum of Art, Tampa, Florida

Philip Evergood, 1901–1975, *Love on the Beach*, 1937. Oil on canvas, 30¼" × 37½" (77.5 × 95.3cm). Hunter Gallery of Art, Chattanooga, Tennessee. Gift of the Benwood Foundation

Jackson Pollock, 1912–1956, *Blue (Moby Dick)*, c. 1943. Gouache and ink on composition board, 18¾" × 23⅞" (47.6 × 60.7cm). Ohara Museum of Art, Kurashiki, Japan

Milton Avery, 1885–1965, *Dunes and Sea II*, 1960. Oil on canvas, 51⅞" × 72" (131.8 × 182.9cm). Whitney Museum of American Art, New York. 50th Anniversary Gift of Sally M. Avery P.14.80

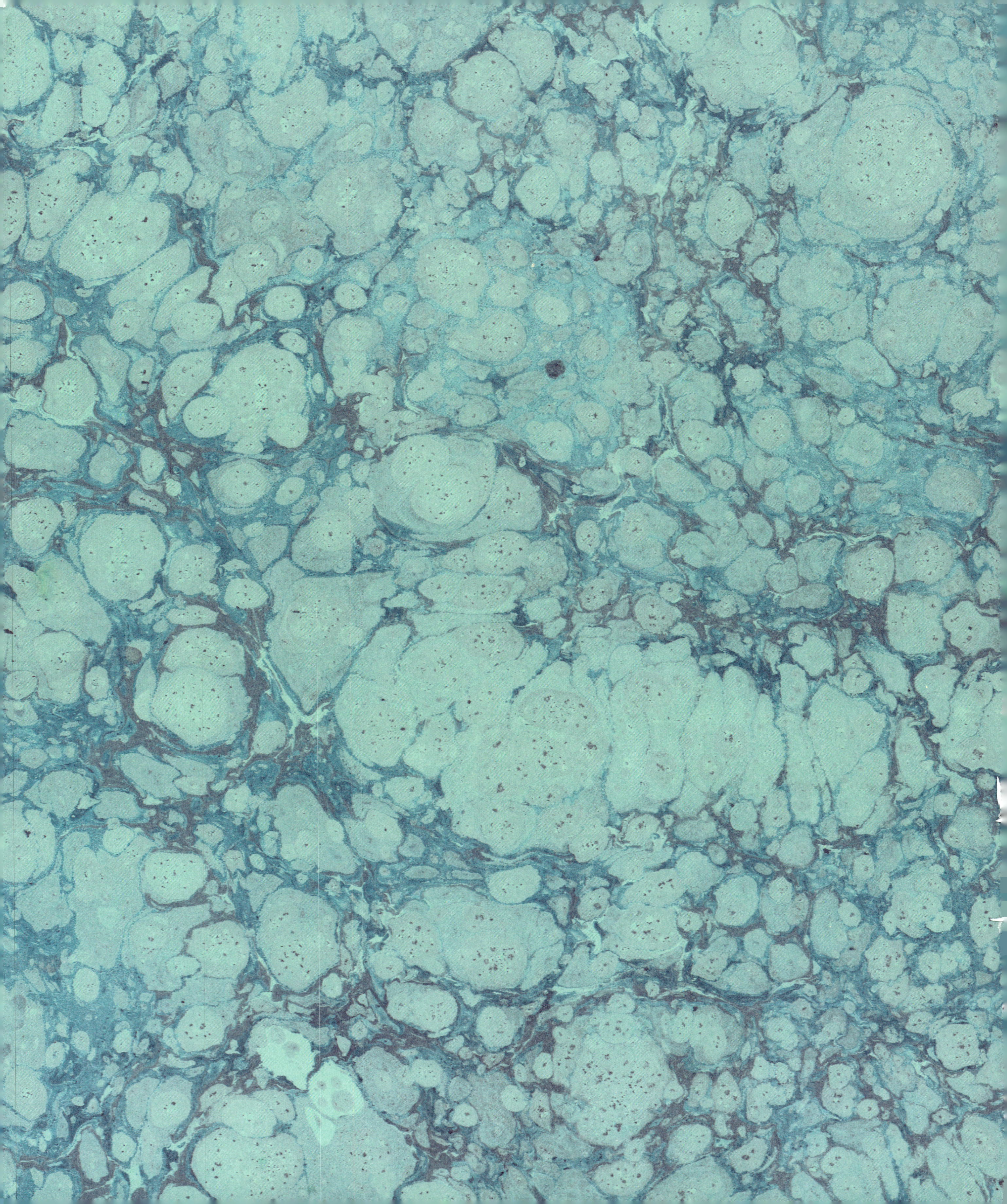